UNCOVER THE SIMPLE PATH TO WEALTH AND NAVIGATING THE PSYCHOLOGY OF MONEY

CULTIVATING THE MINDSET FOR PROSPERITY AND HAPPINESS THROUGH PRACTICAL WISDOM AND BEHAVIORAL INSIGHTS

Daniel Harvey

Preface

Have you ever stood at the edge of a financial precipice, peering into the abyss of uncertainty and fear, wondering if there's a way out? This isn't just a story. It's *your* story, one that begins in the throes of financial despair but leads to a destination of wealth, understanding, and profound personal growth.

Meet Jordan, a figure emblematic of ambition yet burdened by the chains of financial missteps. A vibrant personality in their early thirties, Jordan's journey through the maze of wealth creation is both a cautionary tale and a beacon of hope for anyone feeling lost in the wilderness of personal finance.

It all began on a crisp autumn morning when Jordan, staring at a glaring screen full of red numbers, realized the depth of their financial plight. Debt, like a relentless shadow, had crept into every corner of their life, fuelled by a series of uninformed decisions and a relentless pursuit of instant gratification. This moment, as painful as it was, became the catalyst for a transformation that few could have predicted.

Jordan's first step on the path to financial redemption was a deep dive into the psychology of money. They discovered that their spending habits were not just transactions but emotional decisions, each purchase a band-aid for deeper, unaddressed issues. This revelation was painful but necessary, a foundational lesson on the simple path to wealth. Through stories of individuals who had turned their financial lives around, Jordan found not just inspiration but a mirror reflecting their potential future.

As Jordan embarked on the journey of restructuring their finances, they stumbled upon the concept of "The Simple Path to Wealth" and how adopting a long-term perspective in financial matters could be transformative. Jordan learned about the power of compounding interest, the importance of investing in low-cost index funds, and the wisdom of living below their means. Each chapter of this newfound guide was a step away from the brink and toward a future they had once thought impossible.

But knowledge alone wasn't enough. Jordan's transformation required action. They began by setting clear, achievable goals. Debt repayment became their first milestone, followed by building an emergency fund. Investing was the next frontier, a realm once shrouded in mystery but now demystified through the stories and strategies shared by those who had walked this path before.

Jordan's journey was not without its setbacks. The road to wealth is rarely straight, and they faced their share of challenges, from unexpected expenses to the seductive lure of old spending habits. Yet, it was in these moments of struggle that Jordan's resolve was tested and ultimately strengthened.

The book delves deeper into the strategies for growth, exploring advanced investment options and the psychological resilience needed to navigate the volatile waters of the stock market. Jordan, once overwhelmed by the mere thought of investment portfolios, now found themselves engaged in discussions about risk tolerance and asset allocation with the confidence of an experienced investor.

But the story of wealth is incomplete without exploring the impact of money on one's well-being and relationships. Jordan learned the hard way that wealth for wealth's sake is an empty pursuit. The chapters on "Wealth for Wellbeing" and "The Psychology of Forgiveness in Business" provided not just financial advice but a blueprint for living a balanced, fulfilling life.

The narrative takes a poignant turn as it weaves in the spiritual wisdom of forgiveness. Jordan discovered the liberating power of forgiving not just others but themselves for past financial missteps. This chapter, inspired by biblical stories and real-life tales of forgiveness, became a cornerstone of Jordan's personal growth.

As Jordan's financial health improved, so did their outlook on life. The chapter "Giving Back: The Ultimate Investment" resonated deeply with Jordan, who now saw their wealth not as a means to an end but as a tool for making a difference in the world. The stories of philanthropists who had used their wealth to create lasting impact inspired Jordan to explore impact investing, a way to align their financial goals with their values.

The book closes on a powerful note with "Your Path Forward," a chapter that encourages the reader to reflect on their journey and look ahead to the future. For Jordan, this meant setting new goals, not just for financial growth but for personal development and community engagement.

But the story doesn't end here. As Jordan stands on the precipice of a new chapter, a decision looms that could change everything. Will they take the safe path, ensuring a comfortable but predictable future, or will they leap into the unknown, risking it all for a dream that's just within reach?

This cliffhanger leaves you, the reader, at a crossroads, much like Jordan. The path to wealth and understanding is fraught with challenges, but it's also lined with opportunities for growth, healing, and transformation. Your journey is just beginning. Where will it take you?

Contents

INTRODUCTION

I magine standing at the crossroads of your financial future, where every decision feels like a gamble, and the path ahead is shrouded in mist. This isn't just a metaphor for the uncertain journey of wealth creation; it's the lived reality for many of us as we navigate the complexities of personal finance, investment, and the quest for a fulfilling life. "Uncover The Simple Path to Wealth and Navigating The Psychology of Money" is not just a book; it's a compass, a guide designed to illuminate that path, revealing the steps to financial freedom and psychological well-being.

This book is born out of a simple realization: wealth and happiness are not destinations but journeys marked by growth, learning, and the capacity to navigate the emotional landscape of money. It is penned from a place of deep understanding and empathy, acknowledging that the road to financial independence is as much about managing your money as it is about managing your mind and heart.

From the outset, we dive into the heart of the matter – the psychology of money. It's a fascinating exploration of how our upbringing, beliefs, and emotions shape our financial decisions, often in ways we're not consciously aware of. This book peels back the layers of financial behavior, offering insights into how we can rewrite our money stories to foster wealth and well-being. It's about understanding that every dollar saved, spent, or invested carries the weight of our hopes, fears, and dreams.

As we journey through the pages, we encounter the simple path to wealth, a concept that demystifies the world of finance, stripping away the complexity to reveal the core principles that anyone can follow. It's about seeing through the noise of market fluctuations, investment trends, and the latest financial products to focus on what really matters: building a solid foundation that can weather any storm. This part of the book is both a practical guide and a philosophical treatise on the power of simplicity in achieving financial success.

But this book is more than just a manual for wealth accumulation; it's a narrative woven with real-life stories that breathe life into the principles discussed. These stories, drawn from a diverse tapestry of experiences, highlight the triumphs and trials on the road to financial independence. They serve as both cautionary tales and beacons of hope, illustrating that while the journey is universal, the path is personal.

As the narrative unfolds, we delve into the strategies for growth, examining the tools and techniques for building wealth over the long term. This section is grounded in the understanding that true wealth is not just about the size of your bank account, but about achieving a balance that lets you live your best life. It's here that we explore the delicate dance of risk and reward, the importance of diversification, and the art of making money work for you.

Yet, the pursuit of wealth is not without its pitfalls. The book addresses the psychological hurdles that can derail our financial goals, from the allure of instant gratification to the paralysis of decision-making in the face of too many options. It offers strategies for overcoming these obstacles, emphasizing the importance of resilience, discipline, and a growth mindset.

In a departure from traditional financial advice, the book also ventures into the realms of forgiveness and giving back. It posits that financial freedom is not just about accumulating wealth but about cultivating a spirit of generosity and understanding. The chapters on forgiveness draw on biblical wisdom and personal anecdotes to reveal how letting go of past financial mistakes and grievances can open the door to new opportunities for growth and fulfillment.

As we approach the culmination of this journey, the book challenges us to redefine our relationship with money, urging us to view it not as an end in itself but as a means to create a life of purpose and meaning. It's a call to action to use our financial resources to make a positive impact in the world, whether through philanthropy, ethical investing, or simply by making choices that reflect our values and aspirations.

In the final chapters, "Your Path Forward," the book offers a roadmap for integrating the lessons learned into a coherent strategy for financial and personal growth. It's about setting intentions, making informed choices, and taking deliberate steps towards the life you envision. This section is both a conclusion and a beginning, marking the end of one journey and the start of another.

As you turn the pages of this book, you embark on a voyage of discovery that goes beyond dollars and cents. It's a journey that challenges you to explore the depths of your relationship with money, to confront your fears and desires, and to take control of your financial destiny. But more than that, it's an invitation to join a community of seekers, individuals who are navigating their own paths to wealth and well-being, guided by the shared belief that the best investment we can make is in ourselves.

This book is your companion on that journey. It doesn't promise quick fixes or secret formulas but offers wisdom, insight, and encouragement to help you forge your own path to financial freedom and personal fulfillment. So, as you stand at the crossroads, know that you don't have to walk this path alone. Let "Uncover The Simple Path to Wealth and Navigating The Psychology of Money" be your guide, your mentor, and your inspiration as you embark on this transformative journey.

Remember, the path to wealth and understanding is not just about reaching a destination but about the lessons learned, the growth experienced, and the joy found along the way. As you turn each page, let the stories, strategies, and insights inspire you to take the next step, to dream bigger, and to create the life you've always imagined. This is not just a book; it's a journey to the heart of what it means to be truly wealthy, in every sense of the word. Welcome to the beginning of your new path.

Part I:

Foundations of

Wealth

Chapter 1

The Journey Begins

In business, as in chess, you must always be thinking several moves ahead to stay ahead of the competition.

— Tim Cook

The journey to financial freedom is much more than a quest for wealth; it's a voyage of self-discovery, resilience, and transformation. As we embark on this journey together, I invite you to delve into the very essence of what it means to be wealthy. This chapter isn't just about the mechanics of money management; it's about redefining wealth in a way that resonates with your deepest values and aspirations.

The Philosophy of Wealth: Understanding Money Beyond Numbers

Wealth, in its truest form, transcends the mere accumulation of assets and figures in a bank account. It's about the freedom to live your life on your terms, to pursue your passions without financial constraints, and to create a legacy that extends beyond material possessions. My understanding of wealth has evolved over the years, shaped by personal experiences and the stories of those who've embarked on this journey before me.

I remember sitting down with my mentor, a self-made millionaire who had navigated the tumultuous waters of financial markets to build a formidable portfolio. Yet, when I asked him what wealth meant to him, his answer surprised me. He spoke not of his luxurious home or exotic cars but of the peace of mind he'd achieved, the ability to support causes dear to his heart, and the time he could spend with his loved ones. This conversation was a pivotal moment in my journey, shifting my focus from pursuing wealth as an end goal to viewing it as a means to enrich my life and the lives of those around me.

Mindset Over Matter: Cultivating a Wealth Mindset

The foundation of any significant transformation lies in the mindset we adopt. A wealth mindset isn't just about believing in your capacity to accumulate wealth; it's about embracing the principles of abundance, resilience, and continuous growth. This mindset shift was a game-changer for me, propelling me from a state of financial stagnation to one of proactive wealth creation.

Adopting a wealth mindset began with letting go of limiting beliefs that had held me back. I had to confront the deep-seated notion that financial success was reserved for a select few and that my background predetermined my financial future. This process was neither quick nor easy, but it was essential for breaking the cycle of scarcity thinking that had kept me from realizing my potential.

One of the most profound lessons in cultivating a wealth mindset came from an unlikely source. Sarah, a friend who had overcome staggering debt, shared her journey with me. She spoke of the sleepless nights and the weight of financial uncertainty that had once defined her life. Yet, it was her unwavering belief in her ability to turn her financial situation around that struck a chord with me. Sarah's story was a testament to the power of a wealth mindset; she had not only cleared her debt but had also built a thriving business that allowed her to live her dream life. Her transformation was a vivid reminder that our financial destiny is shaped by our beliefs and actions.

True Stories of Transformation: From Debt to Financial Freedom

The path from debt to financial freedom is both challenging and rewarding. It's a journey marked by setbacks and victories, lessons learned, and obstacles overcome. The stories of those who've navigated this path are a source of inspiration and insight for anyone looking to transform their financial reality.

One such story is that of Michael, a colleague who found himself buried under a mountain of debt after a series of unfortunate investments and unchecked spending habits. The pressure of his financial obligations was a constant source of stress, casting a shadow over his relationships and personal well-being. Michael's journey to financial freedom began with a commitment to change, a willingness to confront his financial mistakes, and the courage to take responsibility for his future.

Through meticulous budgeting, strategic debt repayment, and a disciplined approach to spending, Michael gradually reclaimed control over his finances. But it was his decision to invest in his financial education that truly turned the tide. By learning the principles of effective money management and investment, Michael not only freed himself from debt but also built a robust financial portfolio that provided him with the security and freedom he had longed for.

His story, like many others, underscores the transformative power of resilience, education, and action in the journey to financial freedom. It's a reminder that while the road may be fraught with challenges, the destination—a life of financial independence and peace of mind—is well within reach for those willing to embark on the journey.

As we move forward in this book, remember that your journey to financial freedom is unique, shaped by your personal experiences, goals, and aspirations. The principles and strategies shared here are meant to guide and inspire you, but it's your actions, resilience, and mindset that will ultimately determine your success.

Let this chapter serve as the starting point of your transformation—a call to embrace the philosophy of wealth, cultivate a wealth mindset, and embark on the path from debt to financial freedom. Your journey begins now, and the possibilities are limitless.

Key Points

1. **Understanding Fear and Anxiety:** Acknowledge and recognize the fears and anxieties surrounding wealth-building, including fear of failure, fear of uncertainty, fear of inadequacy, and fear of loss.
2. **Shifting Mindset:** Embrace a growth mindset that views challenges as opportunities for growth and learning rather than insurmountable obstacles.
3. **Education and Empowerment:** Seek knowledge and education about financial matters to empower yourself to make informed decisions and overcome fears rooted in ignorance or misinformation.
4. **Setting Realistic Goals:** Set clear, achievable goals for your financial journey, breaking them down into manageable steps to reduce overwhelm and anxiety.
5. **Cultivating Resilience:** Cultivate resilience by learning from setbacks and failures, understanding that they are natural parts of the journey to success, and developing strategies to bounce back stronger.

Takeaways

1. **You Are Not Alone:** Understand that fears and anxieties about wealth-building are common and shared by many, including successful individuals.
2. **Fear Is a Normal Reaction:** Recognize that fear is a natural response to stepping out of your comfort zone and embarking on a new journey.

3. **Knowledge Is Power:** Educate yourself about financial matters to gain confidence and empowerment in navigating the complexities of wealth-building.
4. **Embrace Challenges:** Embrace challenges and setbacks as opportunities for growth and development rather than reasons to give up.
5. **Start Small:** Begin your journey with small, manageable steps, gradually expanding your comfort zone and building confidence along the way.

Transformative Exercises

1. **Fear Journaling:** Write down your fears and anxieties related to wealth-building in a journal, then challenge each fear by questioning its validity and exploring alternative perspectives.
2. **Visualization:** Visualize yourself overcoming your fears and achieving your financial goals, imagining the feelings of confidence, empowerment, and success.
3. **Affirmations:** Create positive affirmations that counteract your fears and anxieties, such as "I am capable of achieving financial success" or "I embrace challenges as opportunities for growth."
4. **Risk Assessment:** Conduct a thorough risk assessment of your financial goals and strategies, identifying potential obstacles and developing contingency plans to address them.

5. **Action Planning:** Break down your financial goals into actionable steps, prioritizing tasks based on urgency and importance, and create a timeline for implementation.

Reflective Questions

What specific fears or anxieties are holding me back from pursuing my financial goals?	How have past experiences or beliefs contributed to my current fears and anxieties about wealth-building?

_____
_____
_____
_____
_____
_____
_____
_____
_____
_____
_____
_____
_____
_____
_____
_____
_____
_____
_____

_____
_____
_____
_____
_____
_____
_____
_____
_____
_____
_____
_____
_____
_____

What steps can I take to educate myself and increase my confidence in managing financial matters?	What strategies have I used in the past to overcome challenges and setbacks, and how can I apply them to my financial journey?

_____
_____
_____
_____
_____
_____
_____
_____

_____
_____
_____
_____
_____
_____
_____
_____
_____
_____
_____
_____
_____
_____
_____

What support systems or resources can I leverage to help me navigate and overcome my fears and anxieties about wealth-building?

_____
_____
_____
_____
_____
_____
_____
_____
_____
_____
_____
_____
_____
_____

Chapter 2

The Psychology of Money

"Success in business is not just about making money, but also about making a positive impact."

— Warren Buffett

Understanding the intricate dance between our emotions and financial decisions is pivotal in navigating the path to wealth. This chapter delves into the psychological underpinnings of money management, exploring how our feelings influence our financial choices, the critical role of patience in a world obsessed with instant gratification, and the lessons we can learn from successful investors who've mastered their psychological game.

Emotional Finance: How Feelings Influence Financial Decisions

My journey into the world of emotional finance began on a day I'll never forget. I found myself staring at a significant loss in my investment portfolio, a direct result of a panic-driven decision to sell during a market dip. This experience was a harsh but necessary lesson in the power of emotions over financial judgment. It led me to explore the field of behavioral finance, which seeks to understand how psychological influences and biases affect the financial behaviors of investors and financial practitioners.

The stories of individuals who've navigated these emotional waters are both enlightening and sobering. Take, for instance, Emily, a friend who had a penchant for luxury shopping whenever she felt down or stressed. This emotional spending was a temporary balm for deeper issues, leading to a cycle of debt and regret. Emily's journey to financial wellness began with acknowledging the emotional triggers behind her spending habits. Through budgeting, mindful spending, and seeking healthier emotional outlets, she gradually transformed her relationship with money. Her story is a testament to the fact that understanding and managing our emotional responses to money is crucial in achieving financial health.

The Power of Patience: Long-Term Thinking in a Short-Term World

Living in a society that prizes instant gratification, it's easy to lose sight of the long-term perspective essential for building lasting wealth. My own impatience was a barrier I had to overcome early in my investing journey. The allure of quick wins and the frustration with slow progress often led me to make hasty decisions, jeopardizing my financial goals.

The power of patience became evident to me through the story of Thomas, a mentor whose approach to investing was rooted in patience and discipline. Thomas had a knack for looking beyond the immediate fluctuations of the market, focusing instead on the bigger picture. His portfolio, built on a foundation of carefully chosen investments, grew steadily over the years, unaffected by the market's volatility. Thomas taught me that patience is not just a virtue but a strategic asset in investing. It's about making informed decisions, setting realistic expectations, and giving your investments the time they need to mature.

Learning from Legends: Psychological Strategies of Successful Investors

The greatest lessons in the psychology of money come from those who've navigated the financial markets with remarkable success. These legends of investing, such as Warren Buffett and Charlie Munger, have always emphasized the psychological aspect of investing. Their strategies provide invaluable insights into managing emotions, cultivating patience, and making rational decisions in the face of uncertainty.

Warren Buffett's philosophy of being "fearful when others are greedy, and greedy when others are fearful" underscores the importance of counterintuitive thinking in investing. It's a powerful reminder that successful investing often requires us to go against our natural instincts and the prevailing market sentiment. Buffett's approach is not just about picking stocks; it's about cultivating a mindset that sees beyond the emotional turbulence of the markets.

Charlie Munger, Buffett's long-time partner, espouses the principle of "invert, always invert," urging investors to consider problems from multiple angles, particularly by looking at what could go wrong. This mindset encourages a form of psychological resilience, preparing investors to handle the inevitable ups and downs of the market with grace and strategic foresight.

Drawing from these legends, I've learned that mastering the psychology of money means developing a blend of emotional intelligence, patience, and critical thinking. It's about knowing when to trust your gut and when to seek the counsel of those who've walked the path before you. It's recognizing that financial success is as much about managing your mind as it is about managing your money.

As we close this chapter, remember that the journey to financial freedom is as much a psychological journey as it is a financial one. The stories and strategies shared here are not just lessons in finance; they're invitations to explore and master the emotional landscape of your financial life. By understanding the role of emotions in financial decisions, embracing the power of patience, and learning from the psychological strategies of successful investors, you're laying the foundation for a wealthy, well-balanced life.

1. **Understanding Behavioral Patterns:** Explore the psychological factors that influence financial decision-making, such as cognitive biases, emotional responses, and social influences.
2. **Long-Term Thinking:** Emphasize the importance of adopting a long-term perspective in financial matters, focusing on consistency, patience, and delayed gratification.
3. **Mindset Shift:** Encourage a shift from a scarcity mindset to an abundance mindset, fostering beliefs in abundance, opportunity, and the potential for wealth creation.
4. **Risk Perception:** Examine how individuals perceive and respond to risk, recognizing that risk tolerance varies from person to person and can be influenced by personal experiences and beliefs.
5. **Behavioral Economics:** Introduce concepts from behavioral economics that shed light on irrational financial behaviors and offer strategies for mitigating their impact on wealth-building.

Takeaways:

1. **Awareness is Key:** Recognize the influence of psychological factors on financial decisions and behaviors, and strive to become more aware of your own biases and tendencies.
2. **Patience Pays Off:** Understand that wealth-building is a long-term endeavor that requires patience, discipline, and consistency over time.
3. **Believe in Possibilities:** Cultivate an abundance mindset that sees opportunities for wealth creation everywhere and believes in the potential for financial success.
4. **Manage Risk Wisely:** Learn to assess and manage risk effectively, balancing the potential for returns with the potential for loss and aligning investments with your risk tolerance and financial goals.
5. **Learn from Mistakes:** Embrace failures and setbacks as learning opportunities, recognizing that mistakes are a natural part of the journey to financial success.

Transformative Exercises:

1. **Behavioral Audit:** Conduct a personal audit of your financial behaviors and decision-making processes, identifying any patterns of irrationality or bias.
2. **Visualization Exercise:** Visualize your ideal financial future, imagining yourself achieving your goals and living a life of abundance and prosperity.

3. **Money Mantra:** Develop a positive money mantra or affirmation to counteract negative beliefs or fears about wealth and abundance.
4. **Challenge Your Beliefs:** Challenge limiting beliefs about money and wealth by questioning their validity and exploring alternative perspectives.
5. **Practice Gratitude:** Cultivate a practice of gratitude for your current financial situation and the abundance in your life, shifting your focus from scarcity to abundance.

Reflective Questions:

What psychological factors influence my financial decisions and behaviors, and how do they impact my wealth-building efforts?	How can I cultivate a long-term perspective in my financial planning and decision-making?

_____

What beliefs or attitudes about money and wealth do I hold that may be limiting my potential for financial success?	What strategies can I implement to manage risk effectively and align my investments with my financial goals and risk tolerance?

_____
_____
_____
_____
_____
_____
_____
_____
_____
_____
_____
_____
_____
_____
_____
_____
_____
_____
_____
_____
_____
_____
_____
_____

How can I reframe failures or setbacks as opportunities for growth and learning in my journey to financial success?

_____
_____
_____

Chapter 3

The Simple Path to Wealth

"In the world of business, challenges are opportunities in disguise."

-        Richard Branson

Embarking on the journey to financial freedom can often feel like navigating a labyrinth, with countless paths and overwhelming choices. Yet, through my own ventures and the lessons learned from those who've traversed this terrain before me, I've discovered the profound truth in embracing simplicity. This chapter is a testament to the power of simplicity in building wealth, illustrated through case studies of those who've turned minimalistic strategies into fortunes and concluding with actionable steps to commence your journey today.

The Essence of Simplicity: Why Less Is More in Investing

In my early days of investing, I was drawn to the complexity of financial instruments, believing that sophistication equated to superior returns. This misconception was dispelled after encountering the stories of successful investors who championed simplicity above all. It was a conversation with a seasoned investor, Clara, that illuminated the essence of simplicity for me. Clara, who had amassed significant wealth through investing, shared her philosophy: "Complexity doesn't guarantee success; understanding and patience do." Her portfolio, a model of simplicity, comprised a handful of index funds that mirrored the market's performance. This approach, rooted in the understanding of long-term market trends and compounded interest, minimized fees and maximized returns, debunking the myth that complexity yields greater rewards.

Case Studies: Simple Strategies That Made Millions

The narrative of simplicity in wealth building is echoed in the stories of countless individuals who've turned modest strategies into remarkable fortunes. One such story is that of James, a middle-school teacher with a penchant for frugality and a keen interest in the stock market. James's strategy was simple: invest a portion of his salary each month into a diversified index fund. Over the decades, this uncomplicated approach transformed his modest investments into a multimillion-dollar portfolio. James's story is not one of overnight success but of patience, discipline, and the power of compound interest. It's a compelling illustration of how simplicity, coupled with consistency, can lead to extraordinary wealth.

Another case that stands as a beacon of simplicity's efficacy is that of Maria, who inherited a small sum of money. Rather than diversifying into a complex array of investments, Maria chose to invest her inheritance into a single low-cost index fund. Her decision was met with skepticism from peers chasing higher returns through more intricate means. Yet, years later, Maria's portfolio outperformed many of her peers', reinforcing the notion that simplicity often trumps complexity in the realm of investing.

Building Your Path: Practical Steps to Start Today

Inspired by the principles of simplicity and the success stories of those like Clara, James, and Maria, I embarked on refining my investment strategy, focusing on simplicity and clarity. Herein lies a roadmap to start your journey on the simple path to wealth today:

1. **Educate Yourself**: Begin with understanding the basics of the stock market, the power of compound interest, and the importance of diversification. Resources abound, from books to online courses, that can demystify the principles of successful investing.

2. **Assess Your Financial Health**: Take stock of your current financial situation—your assets, liabilities, income, and expenses. This overview is crucial in crafting a realistic and effective investment plan.

3. **Set Clear Financial Goals**: Define what financial freedom means to you. Whether it's achieving a certain net worth, generating passive income, or saving for retirement, clear goals will guide your investment decisions.

4. **Start Small but Start Now**: The journey to wealth is a marathon, not a sprint. Begin by investing a manageable portion of your income into a diversified index fund or a retirement account like a Roth IRA. The key is consistency, not the amount.

5. **Embrace Automation**: Automate your investments to ensure consistency. Regular contributions to your chosen investment vehicles can simplify your path to wealth and mitigate the temptation to time the market.

6. **Monitor and Adjust**: While simplicity is our mantra, periodic reviews of your investment strategy are essential. Life changes, and so might your financial goals and needs. Adjust your investments accordingly, but always through the lens of simplicity.

The journey to wealth, much like life, is fraught with temptations to veer off the path of simplicity in search of shortcuts and quick wins. Yet, the stories and strategies shared in this chapter underscore the truth that wealth is more often built through simple, consistent actions over time. Embrace simplicity in your investments, celebrate the small victories, and remember that the path to financial freedom is as much about the journey as it is about the destination. Your simple path to wealth begins today, one step at a time.

Key Points:
1. **Simplicity is Key:** Emphasize the importance of simplicity in wealth-building strategies, advocating for straightforward approaches that are easy to understand and implement.
2. **Index Fund Investing:** Introduce the concept of index fund investing as a simple and effective way to build wealth over the long term, emphasizing the benefits of low fees, broad diversification, and market returns.
3. **Avoiding Complexity:** Highlight the pitfalls of complex investment strategies and financial products, advocating for simplicity and transparency in wealth-building approaches.
4. **Staying the Course:** Stress the importance of staying committed to the simple path to wealth, resisting the temptation to chase short-term gains or deviate from proven strategies.
5. **Financial Independence:** Explore the concept of financial independence and how following the simple path to wealth can lead to greater financial freedom and security.

Takeaways:
1. **Keep It Simple:** Understand that wealth-building doesn't have to be complicated; simplicity is often the most effective approach.
2. **Index Funds are Your Friend:** Learn about the benefits of index fund investing and consider incorporating them into your investment strategy for long-term success.
3. **Avoid Overcomplication:** Beware of overcomplicating your financial plan with unnecessary complexity or risky strategies.

4. **Stay Consistent:** Stick to your investment plan and resist the urge to deviate from the simple path, even in times of market volatility or uncertainty.
5. **Focus on Financial Independence:** Keep your eyes on the ultimate goal of financial independence and the freedom it can bring to live life on your own terms.

Transformative Exercises:
1. **Simplify Your Portfolio:** Review your investment portfolio and consider simplifying it by consolidating into low-cost index funds or exchange-traded funds (ETFs).
2. **Automate Your Investments:** Set up automatic contributions to your investment accounts to ensure consistent savings and adherence to your wealth-building plan.
3. **Educate Yourself:** Dive deeper into the principles of index fund investing and financial independence by reading books, listening to podcasts, or attending seminars on the subject.
4. **Create a Financial Independence Plan:** Develop a plan for achieving financial independence, including setting specific goals, creating a budget, and determining your target savings rate.
5. **Track Your Progress:** Regularly review your financial progress and track your net worth over time to stay motivated and accountable to your wealth-building goals.

Reflective Questions:

What fears or anxieties do I have about simplifying my investment approach and following the simple path to wealth?	How can I overcome the temptation to overcomplicate my financial plan and stick to proven, simple strategies?

_____
_____
_____
_____
_____
_____
_____
_____
_____
_____

What steps can I take to educate myself about index fund investing and financial independence, and build confidence in my ability to follow the simple path to wealth?	What specific financial goals do I hope to achieve by following the simple path to wealth, and how will achieving these goals impact my life?

_____
_____
_____
_____
_____
_____
_____
_____
_____
_____

_____
_____
_____
_____
_____
_____
_____
_____
_____
_____
_____
_____
_____

How can I stay disciplined and consistent in my wealth-building efforts, even when faced with uncertainty or market volatility?

_____
_____
_____
_____
_____
_____
_____
_____
_____
_____
_____
_____

Part II:

Strategies for Growth

Chapter 4

Investing with Purpose

"Entrepreneurship is not for the faint of heart; it requires courage, resilience, and unwavering determination."

- Elon Musk

A s I delve into the intricate world of investing with purpose, I'm reminded of the profound impact aligning one's portfolio with life goals can have on one's financial journey. This chapter isn't just about numbers and market trends; it's about crafting a roadmap that reflects our deepest aspirations and values. So, let's embark on this transformative journey together, where each decision is infused with purpose and meaning.

Goal-Oriented Investing: Aligning Your Portfolio with Your Life Goals

Investing without a clear sense of purpose is akin to setting sail without a destination. It's crucial to anchor our investment decisions to our life goals, thereby infusing our financial journey with meaning and direction. As I reflect on my own experiences, I recall the pivotal moment when I took the time to articulate my aspirations into concrete financial objectives. Whether it was envisioning a comfortable retirement, securing financial freedom for my family, or supporting causes dear to my heart, defining these goals provided me with a roadmap to guide my investment strategy.

However, setting goals is just the first step; it's equally important to ensure that they are SMART – specific, measurable, achievable, relevant, and time-bound. This framework not only clarifies our objectives but also enables us to track our progress and adjust our strategy as needed. For instance, instead of merely aiming to "build wealth," I set a specific target of achieving a certain level of passive income by a designated age. This level of specificity allowed me to tailor my investment approach accordingly, whether through dividend-paying stocks, real estate investments, or other income-generating assets.

The Art of Diversification: Finding Your Perfect Balance

Diversification lies at the heart of a resilient investment portfolio, serving as a bulwark against the unpredictable ebbs and flows of the market. Just as a skilled artist blends various colors to create a masterpiece, we must judiciously mix a variety of assets to achieve optimal balance and stability. However, diversification is not merely about spreading investments across different asset classes; it's about thoughtful asset allocation that mitigates risk while maximizing returns.

I vividly recall a period of market turbulence when my diversified portfolio weathered the storm far better than those heavily concentrated in a single asset class. While certain sectors experienced volatility, others remained resilient, underscoring the importance of a well-rounded approach to investing. From equities and bonds to real estate and alternative investments, each asset class plays a distinct role in enhancing portfolio resilience. By embracing diversification, we not only safeguard our investments against market downturns but also seize opportunities for growth across various sectors and industries.

Success Stories: Investors Who Made It Big by Staying True to Their Goals

Behind every successful investor lies a story of perseverance, resilience, and unwavering commitment to their goals. These individuals didn't achieve success by chance; rather, they adhered steadfastly to their vision, navigating obstacles with determination and tenacity. Drawing inspiration from these success stories, I've witnessed firsthand the transformative power of purpose-driven investing.

One such story that resonates deeply with me is that of an entrepreneur who, against all odds, built a thriving business from the ground up. Despite facing numerous setbacks and challenges along the way, including financial hardships and industry disruptions, this individual remained steadfast in their commitment to their long-term goals. Through perseverance, innovation, and a unwavering belief in their vision, they not only overcame adversity but also achieved unparalleled success, inspiring countless others to follow in their footsteps.

As we embark on our own journey of purpose-driven investing, let us draw strength from these stories of resilience and determination. By aligning our portfolio with our life goals, embracing the art of diversification, and drawing inspiration from success stories, we unlock the potential to transform our dreams into reality. So, let's embark on this empowering journey with clarity, conviction, and a steadfast commitment to living a life of purpose and abundance.

Key Points:

1. **Goal-Oriented Investing:** Stress the importance of aligning investment strategies with specific financial goals, whether it's retirement, education, or wealth preservation.
2. **Diversification:** Highlight the benefits of diversifying investment portfolios to mitigate risk and maximize returns over the long term.
3. **Socially Responsible Investing:** Introduce the concept of socially responsible investing (SRI) or environmental, social, and governance (ESG) investing, which allows investors to align their values with their investment decisions.
4. **Impact Investing:** Explore the potential of impact investing, where investors seek to generate positive social or environmental outcomes alongside financial returns.
5. **Risk Management:** Emphasize the importance of managing investment risk through strategies such as asset allocation, diversification, and periodic portfolio rebalancing.

Takeaways:

1. **Set Clear Goals:** Define your financial goals and objectives before making investment decisions to ensure alignment with your long-term aspirations.
2. **Diversify Your Portfolio:** Spread your investments across different asset classes, industries, and geographical regions to reduce risk and enhance overall portfolio stability.
3. **Invest with Purpose:** Consider incorporating socially responsible or impact investing principles into your portfolio to reflect your values and beliefs.

4. **Monitor and Adjust:** Regularly review and adjust your investment strategy as needed to adapt to changing market conditions and evolving financial goals.
5. **Stay Informed:** Stay informed about market trends, investment opportunities, and risk factors to make informed decisions and optimize your investment outcomes.

Transformative Exercises:

1. **Goal Setting:** Take time to clarify your financial goals and objectives, including short-term and long-term aspirations, and prioritize them based on importance and urgency.
2. **Portfolio Analysis:** Conduct a comprehensive analysis of your investment portfolio to assess diversification, risk exposure, and alignment with your financial goals and values.
3. **Research SRI/ESG Funds:** Explore socially responsible or ESG investment funds available in the market and evaluate their performance, investment strategies, and alignment with your values.
4. **Impact Assessment:** Reflect on the potential impact of your investments on society and the environment, and identify opportunities to support causes or initiatives that resonate with you.
5. **Risk Management Plan:** Develop a risk management plan that outlines strategies for mitigating investment risk, including asset allocation, diversification, and contingency planning.

Reflective Questions:

What fears or anxieties do I have about investing, and how are they impacting my ability to achieve my financial goals?	How can setting clear investment goals and objectives help alleviate my fears and uncertainties about investing?

_____
_____
_____
_____
_____
_____
_____
_____
_____
_____
_____
_____
_____
_____
_____
_____
_____
_____
_____
_____
_____
_____
_____

What role do my values and beliefs play in shaping my investment decisions, and how can I align my investments with my personal values?	What steps can I take to diversify my investment portfolio and reduce my exposure to investment risk?

_____
_____
_____
_____
_____
_____
_____
_____
_____
_____
_____
_____

How do I envision the impact of my investments on society
and the environment, and what actions can I take to invest
with purpose and make a positive difference?

_____
_____
_____
_____
_____
_____
_____
_____
_____
_____
_____

Chapter 5

Risk, Reward, and Resilience

"The key to success in business is not to follow the crowd, but to carve your own path."

– Steve Jobs

In the realm of investing, the triad of risk, reward, and resilience forms the cornerstone of any successful financial journey. My path through this landscape has been anything but linear, marked by moments of both triumph and tribulation. It's a narrative shared by many, a testament to the universal nature of our financial endeavors. This chapter delves into the essence of risk management, the pursuit of rewards that align with our sleep-at-night comfort level, and the power of resilience through the storms of financial setbacks.

Understanding Risk: How to Embrace It Wisely

My introduction to the concept of risk came early in my investing career, a harsh lesson learned from a venture that promised high returns but faltered under the weight of unrealistic expectations. It was a pivotal moment that shaped my understanding of risk—not as an adversary but as a constant companion on the journey to financial growth.

Embracing risk wisely begins with self-awareness. Knowing your risk tolerance is akin to understanding your own heartbeat; it's personal, intrinsic, and vital. I learned to assess my comfort level with volatility, to differentiate between short-term fluctuations and long-term potential. This understanding was deepened through the story of Linda, a friend who ventured into the high-risk world of startup investments. Linda's journey was fraught with uncertainty, but her meticulous research and unwavering belief in the startups' potential paid off, transforming her initial investment into a substantial portfolio. Her story underscored the importance of informed risk-taking, a balance between courage and caution

.

The Reward Factor: Maximizing Returns While Sleeping Soundly

The pursuit of reward, while inherently tied to the acceptance of risk, requires a strategy that allows for peace of mind. My quest for this balance led me to the concept of value investing, a principle championed by legends like Warren Buffett. It's an approach that focuses on long-term gains, investing in companies with solid fundamentals that are undervalued by the market.

The reward factor is not just about the financial returns but also about the quality of life and peace of mind it brings. I found my equilibrium through a diversified portfolio that provided steady growth with manageable volatility, allowing me to sleep soundly regardless of market conditions. This approach was mirrored in the journey of Sam, a colleague who had weathered the dot-com bubble by sticking to his principles of value investing. Despite the hysteria that led many to speculative investments, Sam's patience and discipline were rewarded as he emerged from the turmoil with his investments not only intact but poised for significant growth as the market stabilized.

Overcoming Setbacks: Inspirational Comeback Stories

The path to financial success is often punctuated by setbacks, each serving as a crucible for growth and resilience. My own experience with financial loss was a defining moment, forcing me to reevaluate my strategy and reaffirm my commitment to my financial goals. It was a period of introspection and, ultimately, transformation.

The stories of resilience in the face of adversity are numerous, but one that stands out is that of Emily, a friend who experienced significant losses during the financial crisis of 2008. Emily's journey from the brink of financial ruin back to stability and growth is a powerful narrative of resilience. She doubled down on her commitment to financial education, refined her investment strategy, and gradually rebuilt her portfolio. Emily's comeback is a testament to the indomitable spirit of the investor who refuses to be defined by their setbacks.

Her story, and countless others like it, highlight the three fundamental truths at the heart of investing: understanding and embracing risk, seeking rewards that allow for peace of mind, and cultivating the resilience to overcome inevitable setbacks. These principles form the bedrock of a strategy that is not only geared towards financial success but also towards personal growth and fulfillment.

As we close this chapter, let us remember that the journey through risk, reward, and resilience is not a solitary trek but a shared voyage. The lessons learned, both personal and from those who have navigated these waters before us, are beacons that light our way. In embracing risk wisely, seeking rewards that align with our deepest values, and rising with resilience in the face of setbacks, we forge a path that is uniquely our own, marked by growth, achievement, and the profound satisfaction of a journey well-traveled.

Key Points:

1. **Understanding Risk:** Educate readers about the different types of investment risks, including market risk, inflation risk, and liquidity risk, and how they can impact investment outcomes.
2. **Maximizing Returns:** Explore the relationship between risk and reward, highlighting that higher returns often come with higher levels of risk, and encourage readers to assess their risk tolerance accordingly.

3. **Risk Management Strategies:** Introduce various risk management strategies, such as diversification, asset allocation, and dollar-cost averaging, to help mitigate investment risks and enhance portfolio resilience.
4. **Resilience in Investing:** Stress the importance of resilience in navigating the ups and downs of the market, emphasizing the need to stay calm, patient, and disciplined during periods of volatility.
5. **Learning from Setbacks:** Encourage readers to view setbacks and losses as learning opportunities, rather than failures, and to use them as fuel for personal and financial growth.

Takeaways:

1. **Risk is Inevitable:** Understand that risk is inherent in investing, and while it cannot be eliminated entirely, it can be managed effectively through informed decision-making and risk mitigation strategies.
2. **Balance Risk and Reward:** Strive to strike a balance between risk and reward that aligns with your financial goals, risk tolerance, and investment horizon.
3. **Stay Calm and Patient:** Cultivate resilience and emotional discipline to weather market fluctuations and setbacks without succumbing to fear or panic.
4. **Diversify Your Portfolio:** Spread your investments across different asset classes, industries, and geographical regions to reduce concentration risk and enhance portfolio resilience.
5. **Continuous Learning:** Commit to ongoing education and self-improvement in the realm of investing, learning from both successes and failures to become a more knowledgeable and skilled investor.

Transformative Exercises:

1. **Risk Assessment:** Conduct a thorough assessment of your investment portfolio to identify potential risks and develop strategies for managing and mitigating them.
2. **Scenario Planning:** Create hypothetical scenarios to simulate various market conditions and assess the impact on your portfolio, helping you prepare for different risk scenarios.
3. **Stress Testing:** Stress test your investment strategy by analyzing its performance under extreme market conditions, identifying weaknesses, and making adjustments as necessary.
4. **Resilience Building:** Practice resilience-building exercises, such as mindfulness meditation, journaling, or visualization, to cultivate emotional strength and fortitude in the face of adversity.
5. **Post-Mortem Analysis:** Conduct a post-mortem analysis of past investment decisions and outcomes, extracting valuable lessons learned and identifying areas for improvement in risk management and decision-making.

Reflective Questions:

What fears or anxieties do I have about investment risk, and how are they impacting my decision-making process?	How well do I understand my own risk tolerance and capacity for loss, and how can I align my investment

	strategy accordingly?

_____
_____
_____
_____
_____
_____
_____
_____
_____
_____
_____
_____
_____
_____
_____
_____
_____
_____
_____
_____
_____
_____
_____
_____
_____
_____
_____
_____
_____

What risk management strategies am I currently employing in my investment portfolio, and how effective are they in mitigating potential risks?	How do I respond to market volatility and setbacks, and what steps can I take to enhance my resilience and emotional discipline as an investor?

_____
_____
_____
_____
_____
_____
_____
_____
_____
_____
_____
_____
_____
_____
_____
_____
_____
_____
_____
_____

_____

_____

_____

What lessons have I learned from past investment setbacks or losses, and how can I use them to improve my risk management approach and investment decision-making in the future?

_____

_____

_____

_____

_____

_____

_____

_____

_____

_____

_____

Chapter 6

Advanced Wealth-Building Strategies

"Failure is not the end of the road in business; it's just a detour on the journey to success."

- Jeff Bezos

Embarking on a journey of financial enlightenment, I've traversed the foundational landscapes of saving, budgeting, and basic investing. Yet, the horizon of wealth extends far beyond these initial steps, leading into the realm of advanced strategies that promise not just growth but a profound transformation of one's financial destiny. This chapter is a voyage into the deeper waters of wealth creation, guided by lessons from the affluent and strategies refined through personal experience and observation.

Beyond the Basics: Exploring Alternative Investments

The conventional wisdom of stock and bond investments was merely the gateway into a broader universe where real estate, commodities, private equity, and cryptocurrencies beckon with the allure of diversification and potential higher returns. My foray into real estate was an eye-opener, revealing the power of leverage and passive income through rental properties. This venture, inspired by a mentor who had amassed a portfolio that weathered economic downturns with grace, illustrated the tangible asset's value and the cash flow it could generate.

Cryptocurrencies and private equity offered a glimpse into the dynamic and high-stakes world of alternative investments. While the volatility of digital currencies was daunting, it also presented unprecedented opportunities for growth. The key was a balanced approach, allocating only a portion of my portfolio to these high-risk, high-reward ventures, ensuring that the foundation of my wealth remained secure in more stable assets.

The Millionaire's Playbook: Lessons from the Wealthy

Interactions with self-made millionaires and diligent study of their public disclosures have uncovered common threads in their investment philosophies. One such principle is the relentless pursuit of knowledge—understanding not only the markets but also the economic and geopolitical landscapes that influence them. Another is the importance of networking, leveraging relationships to uncover opportunities that lie beyond the reach of conventional research.

A pivotal lesson came from a millionaire investor who emphasized the significance of patience and long-term vision. He shared his strategy of "investing in trends, not tips," focusing on sectors and technologies poised for exponential growth over decades, not just years. This approach, while requiring a steadfast commitment and an unwavering belief in one's convictions, has the potential to yield returns that far exceed the market average.

Crafting Your Strategy: Advanced Techniques Simplified

The culmination of these insights has led to the development of a nuanced investment strategy that embraces both traditional and alternative assets. The foundation remains in well-diversified, low-cost index funds, a testament to the enduring wisdom of capturing market returns. Yet, the allocation to alternative investments introduces an element of growth potential and risk mitigation, reflecting the evolved understanding of wealth-building in the modern era.

Risk management has become a more sophisticated practice, employing tools and techniques to protect against downside while remaining open to upside potential. Utilizing options for hedging, exploring tax-efficient investment vehicles, and employing asset location strategies have all become integral to safeguarding and growing wealth.

The journey into advanced wealth-building strategies is not without its challenges, requiring a commitment to continuous education and an openness to adapt to changing market dynamics. Yet, it's a path that promises not just financial growth but a deeper understanding of the complexities and opportunities within the world of investing.

Key Points:

1. **Exploring Alternative Investments:** Introduce readers to alternative investment opportunities beyond traditional stocks and bonds, such as real estate, private equity, and cryptocurrencies.
2. **Risk Management in Advanced Strategies:** Highlight the increased complexity and risk associated with advanced wealth-building strategies and emphasize the importance of thorough due diligence and risk management.
3. **Lessons from the Wealthy:** Study the investment strategies and habits of successful individuals and institutions, extracting valuable insights and principles that can be applied to one's own wealth-building journey.
4. **Tax Optimization:** Explore advanced tax optimization strategies, such as tax-loss harvesting, estate planning, and offshore investing, to minimize tax liabilities and maximize investment returns.
5. **Advanced Techniques Simplified:** Break down complex wealth-building techniques, such as options trading, leverage, and hedging, into simple and understandable concepts for readers to grasp and apply effectively.

Takeaways:

1. **Diversify Your Portfolio:** Consider diversifying your investment portfolio with alternative assets to reduce reliance on traditional stocks and bonds and enhance overall portfolio resilience.
2. **Understand the Risks:** Recognize the increased risk associated with advanced wealth-building strategies and exercise caution when exploring new investment opportunities.
3. **Learn from the Pros:** Study the investment habits and strategies of successful investors and institutions to glean valuable insights and apply them to your own wealth-building approach.
4. **Seek Professional Guidance:** Consider seeking advice from financial advisors or wealth managers with expertise in advanced wealth-building strategies to ensure informed decision-making and risk management.
5. **Start Small:** Dip your toes into advanced strategies gradually, starting with small investments and gaining experience and confidence over time.

Transformative Exercises:

1. **Research Alternative Investments:** Conduct research on different alternative investment opportunities, such as real estate investment trusts (REITs), peer-to-peer lending platforms, and venture capital funds, to identify potential opportunities for diversification.
2. **Simulated Trading:** Use simulated trading platforms or paper trading accounts to practice advanced wealth-building strategies, such as options trading or leveraged investing, without risking real capital.
3. **Case Study Analysis:** Analyze case studies of successful investors or investment firms that have implemented advanced strategies, identifying key

principles and lessons that can be applied to your own wealth-building approach.

4. **Tax Planning Workshop:** Attend a tax planning workshop or seminar to learn about advanced tax optimization strategies, such as tax-efficient investing, retirement account contributions, and charitable giving.

5. **Risk Assessment Exercise:** Conduct a comprehensive risk assessment of potential alternative investments, evaluating factors such as liquidity, volatility, and correlation with existing portfolio holdings, to determine suitability and risk tolerance.

Reflective Questions:

What alternative investment opportunities am I interested in exploring, and how do they align with my financial goals and risk tolerance?	What are the potential risks and rewards associated with advanced wealth-building strategies, and how can I mitigate risks while maximizing returns?

_____
_____
_____
_____
_____
_____
_____

_____

_____

_____

_____

_____

_____

_____

_____

_____

_____

_____

_____

_____

_____

_____

_____

_____

_____

_____

_____

_____

_____

What lessons can I learn from successful investors or institutions that have implemented advanced strategies, and how can I apply	Do I have the necessary knowledge and expertise to implement advanced wealth-building strategies, or do I need to seek

them to my own wealth-building approach?	professional guidance or education?

_____
_____
_____
_____
_____
_____
_____
_____
_____
_____
_____
_____
_____
_____
_____
_____
_____
_____
_____
_____
_____
_____
_____

How can I start incorporating advanced strategies into my investment portfolio gradually, while ensuring proper risk management and due diligence?

Part III:

Beyond Wealth

Chapter 7

The Psychology of Forgiveness in Business

"Innovation is the lifeblood of business; those who embrace change thrive, while those who resist it falter."

— Bill Gates

T he journey through the intricate world of finance and wealth-building is often perceived through the lens of numbers, strategies, and relentless pursuit of success. Yet, one of the most transformative elements in this journey, often overlooked, is the power of forgiveness. This chapter delves deep into the realms of personal development, biblical wisdom, and a revolutionary perspective on wealth, all through the prism of forgiveness.

Healing and Growth: The Power of Forgiveness in Personal Development

My exploration into the power of forgiveness began in the aftermath of a business partnership gone awry. The betrayal I felt when a trusted partner mismanaged our joint funds was not just a financial blow but an emotional one, leaving scars of resentment and mistrust. The road to forgiveness was long and fraught with resistance. Yet, embracing forgiveness opened a pathway to healing, not just for my emotional well-being but for my financial health as well. It was a lesson in letting go of the past to make room for new opportunities and relationships, grounded in a deeper understanding and mindfulness.

This journey of forgiveness was mirrored in the life of Anna, a friend whose startup faced ruin due to deceit from within her team. The bitterness and anger consumed her focus and energy, diverting her from her goals. Through the process of forgiveness, Anna found the strength to rebuild her business, but this time with a foundation of transparency and trust. Her story is a testament to the fact that forgiveness is not a sign of weakness but a powerful catalyst for growth and resilience.

Biblical Wisdom: Stories of Forgiveness and Their Lessons

The concept of forgiveness is deeply rooted in biblical teachings, offering timeless wisdom on the power of mercy and reconciliation. One of the most profound lessons came from the story of Joseph, sold into slavery by his own brothers, only to rise to power in Egypt and later forgive those who wronged him. This story resonated with me during the darkest moments of my financial disputes, serving as a reminder that forgiveness can pave the way for unforeseen prosperity and leadership.

Another biblical narrative that guided me through the process of forgiveness is the parable of the Prodigal Son. It's a tale that highlights not just the forgiveness of a father to his son but also touches on the themes of redemption, love, and the joy of reconciliation. These stories reinforced my understanding that forgiveness, whether in personal life or business, is not about condoning wrongdoing but about liberating oneself from the chains of bitterness, enabling growth and the possibility of a brighter future.

Forgiving Debt: A New Perspective on Wealth

The concept of forgiving debt extends beyond the personal to the financial, offering a radical perspective on wealth and prosperity. Inspired by the biblical year of Jubilee, where debts were forgiven every 50 years, I embarked on a journey to explore the impact of debt forgiveness in modern times. This exploration was personal; after receiving an unexpected inheritance, I was faced with the decision of pursuing legal action against a debtor or considering forgiveness.

Choosing to forgive the debt was a decision that transcended financial loss; it was an investment in peace and an experiment in generosity. This act of forgiveness not only brought relief and gratitude from the debtor, fostering a relationship built on trust and respect, but it also brought an unexpected return on investment. The goodwill generated led to new business opportunities that far outweighed the initial loss.

This experience, and similar stories from others who have chosen the path of forgiving debt, illustrates that wealth is not merely the accumulation of assets but the cultivation of relationships and community. It challenges the conventional wisdom of wealth retention, proposing that sometimes, the act of letting go can yield returns far greater than those of traditional investments.

Key Points:

1. **Healing and Growth:** Explore the transformative power of forgiveness in business, emphasizing its role in promoting healing, fostering resilience, and catalyzing personal and organizational growth.
2. **Emotional Intelligence:** Highlight the importance of emotional intelligence in navigating conflicts and setbacks in business, including the ability to empathize, communicate effectively, and cultivate forgiveness.
3. **Rebuilding Trust:** Discuss strategies for rebuilding trust and repairing damaged relationships in the aftermath of business conflicts or betrayals, emphasizing the role of forgiveness as a catalyst for reconciliation and renewal.
4. **Biblical Wisdom:** Draw insights from biblical teachings on forgiveness and reconciliation, highlighting timeless principles and lessons that can be applied to business contexts.
5. **Forgiving Debt:** Challenge conventional notions of debt forgiveness in business, exploring the potential benefits of forgiveness for both debtors and creditors, including improved mental health, enhanced productivity, and strengthened relationships.

1. **Forgiveness is Empowering:** Understand that forgiveness is a powerful tool for personal empowerment and growth, allowing individuals to release negative emotions and move forward with clarity and purpose.
2. **Communication is Key:** Recognize the importance of open and honest communication in resolving conflicts and fostering forgiveness in business relationships.
3. **Letting Go of Resentment:** Learn to let go of resentment and bitterness towards others, recognizing that holding onto negative emotions only hinders personal and professional growth.
4. **Building Resilience:** Cultivate resilience in the face of business challenges and setbacks by practicing forgiveness and embracing opportunities for growth and learning.
5. **Leading by Example:** Lead by example in business settings by demonstrating forgiveness, empathy, and compassion towards others, creating a culture of trust, collaboration, and innovation.

Transformative Exercises:

1. **Reflection on Past Conflicts:** Reflect on past conflicts or betrayals in business settings and explore your feelings towards those involved, identifying any

lingering resentment or anger that may be hindering your ability to forgive and move forward.

2. **Empathy Building:** Practice empathy-building exercises, such as role-playing or perspective-taking, to better understand the motivations and perspectives of others involved in business conflicts or misunderstandings.

3. **Letter Writing:** Write a forgiveness letter to someone who has wronged you in a business context, expressing your feelings, releasing any pent-up emotions, and extending forgiveness as a gesture of reconciliation and healing.

4. **Mindfulness Meditation:** Practice mindfulness meditation techniques to cultivate inner peace, clarity, and emotional resilience, helping you to let go of negative emotions and embrace forgiveness in business relationships.

5. **Conflict Resolution Workshop:** Attend a conflict resolution workshop or seminar to learn practical strategies and techniques for resolving conflicts and fostering forgiveness in business settings, both as a leader and as a team member.

Reflective Questions:

What fears or anxieties do I have about forgiving	How have past experiences of conflict or

others in business settings, and how are they impacting my ability to cultivate healthy and productive relationships?	betrayal shaped my attitudes towards forgiveness and reconciliation in business relationships?

_____
_____
_____
_____
_____
_____
_____
_____
_____
_____
_____
_____
_____
_____
_____
_____
_____
_____
_____
_____
_____
_____
_____
_____
_____
_____
_____
_____
_____

What steps can I take to cultivate empathy and understanding towards others involved in business conflicts, and how can this contribute to the process of forgiveness and healing?	What role does forgiveness play in promoting trust, collaboration, and innovation in business settings, and how can I incorporate forgiveness into my leadership approach?

_____
_____
_____
_____
_____
_____
_____
_____
_____
_____

How can I leverage biblical wisdom and timeless principles of forgiveness to navigate conflicts and challenges in my business endeavors, fostering personal and organizational growth?

_____
_____
_____
_____
_____
_____
_____
_____
_____
_____
_____
_____
_____
_____
_____
_____
_____
_____

Chapter 8

Wealth for Wellbeing

"A successful business is built on a foundation of trust, integrity, and ethical conduct."

- Indra Nooyi

We often hear that health is wealth, but how often do we consider wealth as a direct investment in our wellbeing? Throughout my journey, I've come to understand that the true essence of wealth lies not in the accumulation of material possessions but in fostering a holistic sense of wellbeing. This chapter delves into the symbiotic relationship between wealth and wellness, exploring mindful spending, and sharing true stories of fulfillment that transcend traditional financial success.

The Wealth-Wellness Connection: Investing in Your Health

My realization of the wealth-wellness connection came during a period of intense work stress, a time when my physical health took a backseat to financial pursuits. It was a wake-up call that led me to reassess my priorities. I learned that investing in your health is the most fundamental form of wealth accumulation. This means prioritizing regular health check-ups, adopting a balanced diet, engaging in physical activity, and not forgetting mental health care, which includes mindfulness practices and adequate rest.

Investing in health insurance, wellness retreats, and even a simple gym membership can yield dividends far greater than any stock portfolio. These investments in health care are not expenses; they are the foundation of a wealthy life. It's a philosophy that reshapes the way we think about wealth, turning our focus towards a more sustainable, health-oriented approach to living.

Mindful Spending: Aligning Your Wealth with Happiness

Mindful spending is about making financial decisions that align with your deepest values, rather than succumbing to impulsive purchases or societal pressures. It's a principle I adopted after experiencing a sense of emptiness despite material success. I started by defining what truly brought me joy and peace. For me, it was experiences over possessions—traveling, learning new skills, and quality time with loved ones.

This shift didn't happen overnight. It required a conscious effort to evaluate each purchase in terms of its ability to contribute to my long-term happiness. Did buying another luxury watch make me happier than investing in a family vacation or a course on personal development? The answer was a resounding no. Mindful spending helped me align my wealth with genuine happiness, transforming my approach to money and its role in my life.

True Wealth Stories: Finding Fulfillment Beyond Finances

Let me share a story that profoundly impacted my view of wealth and fulfillment. It's about Sarah, a successful corporate lawyer who had reached the pinnacle of her career but felt a void that her salary couldn't fill. Sarah decided to take a sabbatical, volunteering in a community program that supported underprivileged children. This experience changed her life. She discovered a passion for teaching and mentorship, eventually leaving her corporate job to found a nonprofit organization focused on education equity.

Sarah's story is a testament to the idea that true wealth is about more than just financial abundance. It's about making a meaningful impact, pursuing passions, and finding fulfillment in ways that money alone cannot provide. Her journey illustrates the transformative power of aligning wealth with personal values and the pursuit of a purpose beyond oneself.

Similarly, my own experiences have taught me that true wealth is not quantified by the balance in your bank account but by the richness of your life experiences, the quality of your relationships, and the impact you have on the world. This realization has guided me towards a more intentional, fulfilling approach to living and investing.

In closing, this chapter is an invitation to rethink the traditional narratives around wealth. It's a call to explore how our financial resources can be used not just for personal gain but as a tool for promoting wellbeing, happiness, and fulfillment. By investing in our health, practicing mindful spending, and seeking fulfillment beyond finances, we can discover a more profound, enriching form of wealth that benefits not only ourselves but also those around us and the generations to come.

5 Key Points

1. **The Integral Connection Between Wealth and Wellness**: Understanding that true wealth encompasses much more than financial assets—it includes physical, mental, and emotional well-being.
2. **Prioritizing Health as an Investment**: Investing in one's health is the most critical form of wealth accumulation, with long-term benefits that surpass any monetary gains.
3. **Mindful Spending for Happiness**: Aligning spending habits with personal values and long-term happiness rather than short-term gratification.
4. **The Power of Fulfillment Beyond Finances**: True wealth is found in fulfillment, purpose, and impact—elements that money alone cannot buy.
5. **Transforming Wealth into Wellbeing**: Leveraging financial success to enhance personal and community well-being, thereby enriching both individual lives and society as a whole.

5 Takeaways

1. **Wealth is Multidimensional**: Recognize that achieving wealth should not come at the expense of your health or happiness. Balance is key.

2. **Invest in Your Well-being**: Regularly investing in your health—through fitness, nutrition, mental health resources, and rest—is crucial for sustained success.
3. **Conscious Consumption**: Practice mindful spending by asking yourself if a purchase contributes to your long-term happiness and aligns with your values.
4. **Seek Fulfillment**: Pursue activities and goals that provide a sense of purpose and fulfillment beyond the accumulation of material wealth.
5. **Give Back**: Use your wealth to make a positive impact on the lives of others, which can provide a profound sense of satisfaction and purpose.

Transformative Exercises

1. **Wellness Investment Plan**: Create a monthly budget dedicated to investments in your health, such as gym memberships, healthy foods, and wellness retreats. Treat these as non-negotiable expenses.
2. **Happiness Alignment Audit**: For one month, track your spending and note each purchase's impact on your happiness. Review and adjust your spending habits to better align with your sources of genuine happiness.
3. **Purposeful Giving Challenge**: Identify a cause you're passionate about and commit to supporting it—whether through volunteering, financial donations, or raising awareness. Reflect on how this giving contributes to your sense of purpose.
4. **Gratitude and Goals Journal**: Daily, write down three things you're grateful for and one goal that aligns with your values and vision of fulfillment beyond finances. This practice fosters positivity and purposeful living.
5. **Mindfulness Meditation**: Engage in daily meditation focusing on abundance and well-being.

This helps manage anxieties about wealth and fosters a mindset of gratitude and contentment.

Reflective Questions:

What does true wealth mean to you, and how does it encompass more than just financial success?	How can investing in your health now contribute to your long-term vision of wealth and well-being?

_____
_____
_____
_____
_____
_____
_____
_____
_____
_____
_____
_____
_____
_____
_____
_____
_____
_____

_____
_____
_____
_____
_____
_____
_____
_____
_____
_____
_____
_____
_____
_____

In what ways might your current spending habits be misaligned with your ultimate sources of happiness and fulfillment?	Can you identify a moment when giving back or contributing to a cause provided you with a deep sense of satisfaction? How can you incorporate more of these moments into your life?

_____
_____
_____
_____
_____

_____

_____

_____

_____

_____

_____

_____

_____

_____

_____

_____

_____

_____

_____

_____

Reflect on your anxieties and fears about achieving wealth. How can shifting your focus from purely financial success to a holistic view of wealth and well-being alleviate these concerns?

_____

_____

_____

_____

_____

_____

_____

Chapter 9

Giving Back: The Ultimate Investment

"The greatest risk in business is not taking any risks at all."

- Mark Zuckerberg

Throughout my journey in accumulating wealth, I've encountered a profound truth that reshaped my entire perspective on success and fulfillment: giving back is not just an act of charity, but the ultimate investment one can make. This chapter explores the enriching experience of philanthropy, the innovative approach of impact investing, and celebrates the lives of philanthropists whose generosity has left an indelible mark on the world.

The Joy of Giving: How Philanthropy Enriches Your Wealth Journey

Philanthropy has been a cornerstone of my wealth journey, transforming not just the lives of those I aim to help but enriching my own life in unimaginable ways. The joy of giving stems from witnessing the tangible impact of your contributions on the lives of others. It's a fulfillment that surpasses any material possession or personal achievement.

My first significant philanthropic endeavor was a scholarship fund for underprivileged students in my hometown. The decision was inspired by my humble beginnings and the financial struggles my family faced. The joy and gratitude expressed by the scholarship recipients were profoundly moving, providing them with opportunities they thought were beyond their reach. This experience taught me that true wealth lies not in what we keep but in what we give away.

Impact Investing: Making a Difference While Making Money

Impact investing has revolutionized the way I view the power of my investments. It's a strategy that seeks to generate social and environmental impact alongside a financial return, proving that it's possible to do well by doing good. My venture into impact investing began with a renewable energy project. It was not just an investment in clean energy but in the future of our planet. The project not only yielded a healthy return but also contributed to reducing carbon emissions. It was a clear demonstration that financial success and positive societal impact could go hand in hand.

The beauty of impact investing lies in its ability to address global challenges such as poverty, climate change, and inequality, through innovative and sustainable solutions. It's a powerful tool for change, offering a new narrative for wealth creation that values both profit and purpose.

Living Legends: The Philanthropists Who Changed the World

The stories of philanthropists who have changed the world are a source of endless inspiration for me. One such legend is that of Andrew Carnegie, a man who came from humble beginnings and became one of the wealthiest individuals in history. Carnegie's philosophy that "the man who dies rich dies disgraced" led him to donate the majority of his fortune to establish libraries, schools, and universities worldwide. His legacy is a testament to the transformative power of giving back.

Another modern-day hero in philanthropy is Melinda Gates. Through the Bill & Melinda Gates Foundation, she has dedicated her life to tackling global health issues and empowering women and girls around the world. Her work is a powerful reminder that philanthropy can drive progress and change on a massive scale.

These living legends exemplify the ultimate investment: investing in humanity. Their stories underscore the impact one individual can make, inspiring a ripple effect that benefits countless lives and future generations.

Closing Thoughts

As I reflect on my wealth journey, the most gratifying moments have not come from the accumulation of wealth but from the opportunities it has provided me to give back. Philanthropy and impact investing have enriched my life with purpose, joy, and a sense of connection to the global community.

Giving back is the ultimate investment, one that yields returns beyond measure. It's an investment in the future, in the betterment of society, and in our shared humanity. As we navigate our paths forward, let us remember that the greatest legacy we can leave is not one of wealth, but of meaningful contributions to a world that so desperately needs it.

This chapter is an invitation to view wealth not just as a means to personal success, but as a powerful tool for making a difference. It's a call to action to leverage our resources, influence, and time to contribute to a more equitable, sustainable, and compassionate world. The journey of giving back is not just the path to true wealth; it's the path to a richer, more fulfilling life.

Key Points

1. **Philanthropy as Personal Growth**: Engaging in giving back is not just beneficial for the recipients but also for the donor, fostering personal growth, gratitude, and a sense of fulfillment.
2. **Impact Investing for Dual Returns**: Impact investing demonstrates that it's possible to achieve both financial return and social impact, challenging the traditional view of wealth accumulation.

3. **The Ripple Effect of Generosity**: Acts of generosity have a cascading impact, benefiting broader communities and future generations, and encouraging a culture of giving.
4. **Diverse Ways to Give Back**: Giving back isn't limited to financial contributions; volunteering time, sharing knowledge, and offering resources are equally valuable.
5. **Legacy of Change**: Philanthropy and social impact investing are powerful tools for creating a lasting legacy that goes beyond wealth.

Takeaways

1. **Giving Is Growth**: Recognize that philanthropy enriches your life, deepening your connection to humanity and enhancing your personal development.
2. **Investments with Impact**: Explore opportunities for impact investing as a means to contribute positively to societal issues while also seeking financial returns.
3. **Generosity Breeds Generosity**: Understand that your acts of giving can inspire others, creating a multiplier effect that extends the reach of your generosity.
4. **Everyone Can Contribute**: No matter the level of wealth, everyone has something to give. Identifying your unique resources can amplify your impact.
5. **Building a Legacy**: Consider how you want to be remembered and what values you wish to pass on. Philanthropy is a key component of a meaningful legacy.

Transformative Exercises

1. **Generosity Plan**: Draft a plan that outlines how you intend to give back, including both financial contributions and non-monetary ways you can make a difference.
2. **Impact Investment Research**: Spend time researching impact investing opportunities. Identify one or two that align with your values and take steps to invest.
3. **Volunteer Day**: Commit to a day of volunteering at a local charity or organization. Reflect on the experience and how it impacts your sense of purpose and connection.
4. **Knowledge Sharing Session**: Host a workshop or seminar in your area of expertise for those who could benefit from your knowledge, contributing to their growth and success.
5. **Legacy Letter**: Write a letter to your future self or a loved one, expressing the values and impact you hope to achieve through your philanthropic efforts.

Reflective Questions:

How does the concept of giving back align with your personal definition of success and fulfillment?	What fears or anxieties do you have about allocating resources (time, money, knowledge) to philanthropy, and how can you address these concerns?

Reflect on a time when someone's generosity made a significant impact on your life. How does this influence your views on giving back?	In what ways can impact investing complement your financial goals while contributing to social or environmental causes you care about?

_____
_____
_____
_____
_____
_____
_____
_____
_____
_____
_____
_____
_____
_____
_____
_____
_____
_____
_____
_____
_____

_____

_____

How do you envision your legacy in terms of
philanthropy and social impact? What steps can you
take now to start building that legacy?

_____

_____

_____

_____

_____

_____

_____

_____

_____

_____

_____

_____

_____

_____

_____

_____

_____

_____

_____

Chapter 10

Your Path Forward

"In business, as in life, it's not the challenges we face that define us, but how we choose to overcome them."

-                    Oprah Winfrey

As I approach the culmination of this narrative, I am compelled to reflect on the essence of what it truly means to carve a path forward. This journey, rich with lessons of success, failure, and resilience, has not only shaped my perception of wealth but also of life itself. In this final chapter, I will delve into the art of crafting a lasting legacy, the significance of continual growth, and share some practical advice for navigating the road ahead.

Crafting Your Legacy: How to Leave a Mark Beyond Money

The concept of legacy has always fascinated me, not as a monument to personal success, but as a beacon that guides future generations. My understanding of legacy was profoundly influenced by the life of my grandmother, a woman who, despite never amassing great wealth, left an indelible mark on our community through her acts of kindness and unwavering support for education.

Inspired by her, I learned early that a true legacy is not quantified by the wealth one accumulates but by the impact one has on the lives of others. Crafting such a legacy requires intentionality, a commitment to live by values that transcend personal gain, and a desire to contribute to the betterment of society. It's about creating something that endures beyond one's lifetime, whether through philanthropy, mentorship, or simply the way we choose to live our lives and inspire those around us.

Continual Growth: Lifelong Learning as an Investor

My journey as an investor has been marked by continuous learning. The landscape of investment is ever-evolving, and success in this field demands an unyielding commitment to education and self-improvement. Early in my career, I faced a significant loss due to a lack of understanding of market dynamics. This experience was a turning point, teaching me the invaluable lesson that knowledge is as crucial an asset as any in my portfolio.

Since then, I've dedicated myself to lifelong learning, embracing every opportunity to broaden my understanding of finance, economics, and emerging trends such as sustainable investing and technological innovations. This commitment has not only enhanced my investment acumen but has also instilled a mindset of adaptability and curiosity, which I believe are essential qualities for any investor.

Next Steps: Practical Advice for the Road Ahead

As we look to the future, the path forward is both exciting and uncertain. Here, I offer some practical advice gleaned from my own experiences and the wisdom of those who have walked this road before me:

1. **Embrace Change:** The only constant in life and investing is change. Embrace it. Being adaptable and open to new ideas will enable you to navigate the complexities of the financial world and life's unpredictability.

2. **Set Clear Goals:** Define what success means to you, beyond the accumulation of wealth. Whether it's achieving financial independence, giving back to your community, or leaving a legacy, having clear goals will guide your decisions and actions.

3. **Invest in Relationships:** Wealth is not solely about financial assets; it's also found in the richness of our relationships. Invest time and energy in building strong connections with family, friends, and mentors. These relationships are invaluable sources of support, wisdom, and joy.

4. **Prioritize Well-being:** Never lose sight of the importance of your physical, mental, and emotional

well-being. Wealth without health is meaningless. Make self-care a priority, ensuring that you're able to enjoy the fruits of your labor.

5. **Give Back:** Consider how you can use your wealth and skills to make a positive impact on the world. Whether through philanthropy, volunteer work, or simply acts of kindness, giving back is one of the most rewarding aspects of wealth.

6. **Stay Humble:** Success can be fleeting, and the journey is often fraught with challenges. Remain humble, learn from your mistakes, and never forget where you came from.

Closing Reflections

As I close this chapter, and indeed this book, I'm reminded of a quote that has guided me through the years: "The greatest use of a life is to spend it on something that will outlast it." Our journey through life and the realm of investing is not just about accumulating wealth; it's about creating a legacy, fostering continual growth, and preparing for the future with wisdom and humility.

The path forward is yours to shape. Armed with the lessons of the past and the promise of tomorrow, may you tread this path with courage, generosity, and an unwavering commitment to your values. Here's to a future that reflects not just the wealth we've accumulated, but the depth of our character and the breadth of our impact on the world.

Key Points

1. **Defining Personal Success**: Success is a personal journey that goes beyond financial riches to include fulfillment, happiness, and a sense of purpose.
2. **The Importance of Continual Growth**: Emphasizing the role of lifelong learning, personal development, and adaptation in sustaining and growing wealth.
3. **Crafting a Meaningful Legacy**: Encouraging readers to think about the legacy they wish to leave, focusing on impact beyond wealth accumulation.
4. **Balancing Wealth with Well-being**: Stressing the importance of maintaining a healthy balance between pursuing wealth and ensuring personal and familial well-being.
5. **Actionable Steps Towards Wealth**: Offering practical advice for wealth accumulation that aligns with personal values and goals.

Takeaways

1. **Personalize Your Success**: Understand that your definition of success should reflect your values, goals, and what makes you genuinely happy.
2. **Commit to Never-Ending Improvement**: Acknowledge the power of continual learning and self-improvement in achieving and maintaining wealth.

3. **Legacy is More Than Money**: Recognize that a meaningful legacy is built through impact, relationships, and the positive change you foster in the world.
4. **Well-being is Wealth**: Remember that true wealth includes health, happiness, and well-being, not just financial assets.
5. **Practical Steps are Key**: Accept that achieving wealth requires actionable steps, disciplined financial planning, and a willingness to take calculated risks.

Transformative Exercises

1. **Success Vision Board**: Create a vision board that represents your personal definition of success, including elements of wealth, well-being, and fulfillment.
2. **Lifelong Learning Plan**: Develop a plan for acquiring new knowledge or skills each year, focusing on areas that will enhance both your personal and professional life.
3. **Legacy Mapping**: Write down the legacy you wish to leave, considering the impact on your family, community, and beyond. Outline steps you can take to start building this legacy now.
4. **Well-being Audit**: Conduct a monthly audit of your life, assessing your physical, emotional, and financial health. Identify areas for improvement and action steps.
5. **Financial Action Plan**: Draft a detailed financial plan that outlines your wealth goals, investment strategies, and milestones. Include a timeline and review it regularly.

Reflective Questions:

How does your current path align with your personal definition of success? What adjustments, if any, are needed to better align with your vision?	What new knowledge or skill can you acquire this year to enhance your ability to create wealth? How does continuous learning play into your long-term wealth strategy??

_____
_____
_____
_____
_____
_____
_____
_____
_____
_____
_____
_____
_____
_____
_____
_____
_____
_____
_____
_____
_____
_____
_____

_____
_____
_____
_____
_____
_____
_____
_____
_____
_____
_____

In reflecting on the legacy you wish to leave, what are the key components that matter most to you? How can you start to build or enhance this legacy today?	How do you balance the pursuit of wealth with maintaining your personal well-being and happiness? Are there areas where you need to make adjustments?

_____
_____
_____
_____
_____
_____
_____
_____
_____

_____
_____
_____
_____
_____
_____
_____
_____
_____
_____
_____
_____
_____

How can I start incorporating advanced strategies into my investment portfolio gradually, while ensuring proper risk management and due diligence?

_____
_____
_____
_____
_____
_____
_____
_____
_____
_____
_____
_____
_____

_____
_____
_____
_____
_____
_____
_____
_____
_____
_____
_____
_____
_____

Acknowledgements

As I turn the final page on the creation of **UNCOVER THE SIMPLE PATH TO WEALTH AND NAVIGATING THE PSYCHOLOGY OF MONEY**, I am filled with a profound sense of gratitude and reflection. This book, a tapestry woven from my personal experiences, insights, and aspirations, would not have been possible without the contribution of many remarkable individuals and the inspiration drawn from a lifetime of learning.

First and foremost, I must express my deepest thanks to the giants upon whose shoulders I stand. Authors such as Brené Brown, whose explorations of vulnerability and strength have illuminated the path to personal growth; Dale Carnegie, whose timeless wisdom in "How to Win Friends and Influence People" continues to shape the art of human connection; and Stephen Covey, whose "7 Habits of Highly Effective People" has been a compass for personal and professional integrity. Their groundbreaking work has not only enriched my life but also motivated me to embark on the journey of writing this book, hoping to echo their impact on the lives of others.

To my family, whose love and support know no bounds, I owe an immeasurable debt of gratitude. To my wife, Bernadette, your unwavering faith in me and your constant encouragement have been the light guiding me through moments of doubt and the joy amplifying our successes. Your partnership is my greatest treasure.

To my mother, Lucy, thank you for instilling in me the values of hard work, perseverance, and compassion. Your sacrifices have not gone unnoticed, and your wisdom has been my guiding star. You taught me that the true measure of success is not in the wealth we accumulate, but in the lives we touch and the love we share.

I am also immensely grateful to the countless friends, mentors, and colleagues who have offered their insights, challenged my perspectives, and celebrated my milestones. Your collective wisdom has been a wellspring of inspiration and a reminder of the strength found in community.

To my readers, I extend my heartfelt thanks. Your willingness to embark on this journey with me, to explore the depths of your own potential, and to strive for a life of purpose and fulfillment is the greatest honor an author could ask for. This book is for you, crafted with the hope that it will serve as a beacon on your path to personal and financial well-being.

In closing, I am reminded that the journey of self-improvement is both personal and universal. As we share our stories, our struggles, and our triumphs, we discover that our dreams are connected by the common threads of human experience. May **UNCOVER THE SIMPLE PATH TO WEALTH AND NAVIGATING THE PSYCHOLOGY OF MONEY** be a companion on your journey, a source of inspiration, and a reminder that the path to a fulfilling life is paved with growth, generosity, and the courage to pursue our highest ideals.

With deepest gratitude,

Daniel Harvey

Scan this QR code to get the free
audio book

www.ingramcontent.com/pod-product-compliance
Lightning Source LLC
Chambersburg PA
CBHW071052290526
45795CB00004B/1453